The Variety Of The Spiritual Awakening

How Some of Us Found Our Way to Jesus

by Charles Paul Stephens
Foreword by Steve and Tricia B.

Outskirts Press, Inc.
Denver, Colorado

Outskirts Press, Inc.
http://www.outskirtspress.com

ISBN: 978-1-4327-2096-4

Outskirts Press and the "OP" logo are trademarks belonging to Outskirts Press, Inc.

PRINTED IN THE UNITED STATES OF AMERICA

With Selections by the following people

Johnette Clark
Natalie Taylor
Dewayne Lunday
Shannon Poole
Shelley Copeland
Steven Howell

DR Banks
Thank You...Sir

Charle Paul Steph

8-24-09

DEDICATION

I cannot begin another work without offering heart-felt & sincere dedications to my dear and loving wife, Linda Sue Stephens. Without her none of this would ever be possible. Her unconditional, AGAPE, love keeps me foreverreaching for more; More God, More Jesus and More Faith. It is her love for me that offers me a picture of God's love for me. Without it I would have never understood Jesus and what He did for all of us- Unconditional, AGAPE forever!

I cannot ever forget the love and support of Steveand Tricia B. of Fort Worth Texas. Not only did they take the time to write the forward, they are my friends, mentors and life examples. I owe them a great debt that I can never repay in this life, so, I must join them in the next to continue payments for my salvation and joy of living.

I cannot forget the first time I heard Pastor Jeff preach. I was amazed at how close he was to my very soul. Jesus used him(Jeff) to demolish the walls I had built around my heart. He used the words of Christ along with his personal experience to fill the void left my drugs and alcohol. I would be amiss to ever leave his name from any book I am blessed to write.

I have not thus far and I feel I will never forget what he did for my dear wife Linda and I. Thank you Pastor Jeff, your wife and your children!

And to our Lord and savior Jesus Christ, please do not forget your humble servants as we continue to try and please You each day. Walk with us, talk with us and offer us wisdom beyond what is deserved. Our Lord Jesus Christ who is the author and finisher of ANY Spiritual Awakening by ANY person.

A debt I cannot pay,
A gift I do not deserve;
Grace is such a wonderful thing.

FOREWORD
BY STEVE AND TRICIA B.
FORT WORTH TEXAS

There is a reason why men build bridges rather than burn them(bridges). In order to get from point A to point B in the quickest manor you should walk a straight line. Without a bridge you would have to go through the mountains and even into thevalleys. If a man knows how to build a bridge, God knows how to build that same bridge in our lives with other people. He teaches how to gothrough life using bridges so that we do not have to go through the valleys where there are so many pitfalls or over the mountains where we will have to struggle to get to the top. Then, try to keep from falling back into the valleys.

The spiritual experiences Big Charlie shares in thisbook are a real testament to his willingness to let God build the bridges he needs to walk on everyday.The spiritual experiences he shares will take you a roller coaster ride because they are real and are the same ones that many of us have to experience in oneway of another, at one time or another. Big Charlie has learned through his spiritual experiences that God has a plan in his life that will keep him on the bridge and out of the valleys or off the mountains.

He has a call on his life placed there by God to share his passion for drawing others closer to Jesus.Big Charlie has learned that he is a spiritual being acting in a human experience. Big Charlie and his dear wife Linda are going to do great things for the Kingdom of God while crossing many more bridges in their lives.

Steve and Tricia B.
Fort Worth Texas

* Steve B. has been my friend, sponsor and mentor for over a decade now. I am not sure where I would be if God had not given me him as a sponsor, first and a friend and mentor next. He encouraged me gently toward Christ in a way that I had never seen.Never condemning, never shaming and in the vision of Christ Himself, always with love and compassion.

Thank you Steve and thank you Tricia for everything!

GRATITUDE

My gratitudes speaks when I care and share my personal experiences with those I meet in life!

With great respect and love I mention these people; My pastor and his wife, Jeff Wickwire of Ft. Worth

My new pastor and his wife, Art Lynch of Dumas

My spiritual advisor and his wife, Gary Hammonds

My son and his wife Kerry Niemann of Austin TX

My newest friends & his family, Brent Clark, Dumas

My dear friend Craig Solomon and his wife, Vega

My daughter, Jamie Owens and her kids, in CA
My dear friends Steve and his wife, Fort Worth TX and
My dear and loving wife Linda Sue Stephens

To each of you, thank you and God bless you for your encouragement and endless compassion. May God see, through me, what you have done for me! And may my gratitude always be a testament to you, and those we all try to help. Thank you all for your love, your prayers and your friendships! May God Bless you all richly in this life and the NEXT!

SPECIAL THANKS AND BLESSINGS

The Childs Family of Ft. Worth

I would never forget the late, great Dan Childs and his wonderful family. They watched over me, prayed for me and supported me in many spiritual walks as I made my path through life. I love them all with all my heart and I know that Dan watches over me today, possibly even more than before. God bless you Dan, Cissy, girls & the entire Childs Family of Fort Worth Texas. As his girls grow up may they always know the love I shared with their father and just how much gratitude I have for this humble man.May they know just how important this man was too who I am today. The Living Room @ The Refuge is built in his honor and memory. Thank you Dan,you are missed every day. And everyday I think of you and wished you were here to see what Jesus has done with your friend! May the God of your under-standing extend a hand of welcome as you enter His **ETERNAL PARADISE**

PREFACE

Purpose.....Calling.....Mission.......Anointing.or possibly an - *Awakening*

Stop playing games with your eternity and pick a name and stick with it! As human beings we try so hard to complicate things(seemingly)so others cannot possibly get a piece of the action. It's no different than Biblical days where the priest and bishops tried to place rules on everyone BUT themselves so they could feel better about just how sick they were. The Bible in it's simplest form is this - A relationship with God through

Jesus Christ! Period!

To truly change, every human being must repent to change. We must turn from what we are doing and begin to do something (anything) differently. This is a spiritual awakening; A change in perception, para dime shift or a moment of clarity, as some of the secular movement would suggest. All it is, is an acceptance of our spiritual nature and awaken to every possibility that entails. That's it, nothing more. We are either spiritual beings or we are not. This is NOT about religion! Today you must chose!

God is a Spirit!

God operates in a spiritual realm. So to be closer to God, we too, must operate in the spirit. We must grow in spirit. We are either alive in spirit or we are dead in spirit; which are you today. As human beings, many of us are dead spiritually. However, like Jesus, we too can be Resurrected. Are you ready to be Born Again as the Bible suggest. Is your Old Man dead and stinking? Are you ready to give birth to a New Man -

A Spiritual Man?

The Spirit of wisdom and of understanding, **The Spirit** of counsel and of power, the **Spirit** of knowledge and of the fear of the LORD The **spirit** is willing, but the body is weak."

Premise
n. **prem·iss** (prĕm'ĭs)
    1.   A proposition upon which an argument is based or from which a conclusion is drawn.
        a. One of the propositions in a deductive argument.
        b. Either the major or the minor proposition of a syllogism, from which the conclusion is drawn.

2.   premises Law The preliminary or explanatory statements or facts of a document

If you believe as I do, then you believe we have soul.If not, then you believe this is _all_, there is no Eternity.

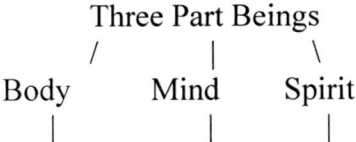

Three Part Beings

```
        /       |       \
   Body      Mind      Spirit
     |         |          |
```

Daily we feed our Body & sometime even our Minds

Yet, most of us NEVER feed our Spirit or Soul

```
      /           |           \
```

Food   **Learning**   **Prayer**

For many of us, our spirits are dying, they are literally starving to death.   That pain, that hole we have in our gut is our spirit begging to be fed. We try to feed it by using drugs, acting out sexually or with fits of anger and rage. In a perverse way, we try to feed our spirit with a food that will NOT fill the spirit as needed. We need God, Prayer and Meditation!

We need an AWAKENING!

QUOTES

"Man lives consciously for himself, but is an unconscious instrument in the attainment of the historic, universal aims of humanity."

Leo Tolstoy
1828 – 1910

On Aug. 28, 1811, John Adams wrote, "Religion and virtue are the only foundations, not only of republicanism and of all free government, but of social felicity under all governments and in all the combinations of human society."

We are trying destroying this world an its inhabitants. Our greed, our thirst, and our hunger for more are infecting the entire race. Each day, more and more Biblical prophecy is being fulfilled, not one or two as with other obscure predictions, but literally hundreds. Folks, these are warnings; warnings of the HELL that is to follow if we do not have a Spiritual Awakening as Jesus Christ meant.

Charles Paul Stephens 1959 - ?

PART ONE

CHAPTER ONE

I had originally thought I would put this in some sort of calender order, and still may. However, I must begin with my definition of the spiritual experience or spiritual awakening. I can go no further, I need not proceed another page if you do not understand the Premise. You do realize that what I am talking about is not necessarily religious or a religious experience. It may have a salvation quality(and does) but as a rule, avoid most religious doctrine. I sincerely believe this is where many people get confused and go wrong in life . Many have sat in church for years and never felt anything. Many have become deacons, ran youth programs, only to be consumed by sin such as gambling, alcohol or pornography. WHY? At the same time many kick the carpet, twist their wedding bands and most (like myself) contemplated the Sunday evening meal over and over. Where was God? More important, where are we? Lost! Attending church without a spiritual awakening is like cooking bread with no yeast; **You Will Never Get A Rise Out of It!**

First, I had to ask God into my life, then I had to immediately make room for Him in my life. Unlike at His birth, Jesus will not stay where there is no room. Asking God to help me, bless me or otherwise save me is silly if I am not going to set aside valuable time for Him. Why would He waste His time is I won't?

Next I had to decide - make a chose - that I wanted to know Him and His plans for my life. Decide implies action, action indicated that I read, pray, meditate or otherwise seek that plan He has for me. Wow, are we really willing to do what is required to have that relationship we speak? No, not at first. In the beginning I played religion just like most everyone else. I sat in the pews, I contem-plated the many dishes on the Chinese Buffet or maybe who would quarterback my favorite team at 2pm. I watched as others received the Holy Spirit, I watched as many found true peace and joy.

I even envied those who were anointed or blessed. What was I doing wrong? Why would God not enter my life and manifest Himself in me? NO ROOM! God wants a relationship, with me , on His schedule. He simply refuses to participate in our Over-rated, under-performed lives that we think are so great.

Make room or Move over.

That all said, I still need to define spiritual awakening. Steve Covey called it a "para dime shift". Rick Warren called it a "Purpose Driven Life". And still others call it everything from awakening to anointing. What we are talking about is an honest, sincere change in our perceptions, attitudes and ideas of life and our part in it.

We must wholly realize that "this life is but a vapor"; a vapor between two eternities. We came from a spiritual eternity and we shall return too a spiritual eternity. This life, this vapor of an existence will determine where you and I spent that final eternity.

Does anyone truly believe that this is all there is or was ever meant to be?

Does anyone actually believe in their heart that there is no life after death?

Does anyone sincerely believe that the Bible is just another book wrote by men?

Way better men than I believe in Heaven (or Hell), so who am I to argue against such things and on what basis do I rest my argument - The ranting of other men whom share nothing of my life?

Come on folks, let's get REAL!

REAL.........REAL

CHAPTER TWO

Jesus Loves the little children , all the little children of the world. They are yellow black and white, they are always in His sight, Jesus loves the little children of the world.

I found comfort in church as they talk about LOVEor the great stories of Moses or Job. Knowing that Jesus loved me was accepted but quite misunder-stood. Not having a father, yet having a mother that seemed to have no idea about LOVE made Jesus' LOVE a mystery of sorts. His LOVE was fleeting at best, in proportion with how I acted or what I did. Once I finally moved into the adult service, oh, about 11 maybe 12 years old, I was consumed with guilt over my illegitimate status as a fatherless child. I was ashamed of the ideas and thoughts that continually race through my brain. I was told (often) that, that was the Lord convicting me, yet, the concept was NEVER explained. Why didn't someone tell me just how much Jesus "loves the fatherless" and "the orphaned"?

Instead, I was told " that to think bad thoughts was just as much a sin as actually doing the deed." How could that be? Was I truly responsible for those thoughts I had no real control over? I could stop doing those seemingly ugly things with those little girls next door but for the life of me I could not stop thinking about them. Why didn't someone let me know that little boys were "just wired that way by God"?

I could avoid their phone calls, I could ignore them at school, but alone, in my room or outside working, I could not stop thinking about just how beautiful they were and some of the things we had done.

No one ever explained just how normal this was although most of it wrong. All I heard was " The wages of sin is death" or " you will go to Hell and burn forever." The educated leaders, the uninformed parents seem to always forget about ;

"Jesus loves the little children, all the little children of the world "

"God so loved the world that He gave His only begotten son......"

And what about Grace? What about the words of Paul , "although I do not do what I want to do, but what I do not want to do is usually what I do". (Romans)Why is it that the shame for sin is usually the avenue that so many take early on?

Parents should realize how important the early stages of child growth really are, especially concerning their spiritual nature and allowing that to bloom. It is my opinion that the moral fiber of a child is woven between the ages of birth and 8. Seriously, a child knows every thing it needs to survive before they ever walk into a school classroom. It is by this time that all children should have a true idea of " RIGHT and WRONG".

Otherwise their fabric, their moral fiber will not with stand the temptations of each day. Having no father, having a very dysfunctional mother and being passed around from one location to another like a terribly bad Fruit Cake at Christmas, left me with no clear idea of "RIGHT and WRONG" and holes torn in my moral fabric. Sins only affect on me was guilt, shame and selfishness - **I was Self-centered.**

"Self-" are part of the American make-up. It means we can act anyway we please with no real consequences. All the while we kill ourselves, one pill, one drink, one buffet, or one sex act at a time. I/We are actually committing Spiritual Suicide. Parents, Preachers and most Police refuse to admit the total importance of early childhood growth. Most focus on the importance "peers" while ignoring the developments aspects of the parents and the church on a child. Who is training a child at 2-3 and 4 years old? A teacher? A baby-sitter or one's own relatives?

The Five P's of Development
        Parents
        Peers
        Preachers

Professors
Police

Our children will learn what they need to know from _one_ of these "P"s!

CHAPTER THREE

Who is smart enough to deny another their own spiritual experience? Who is wise enough to say "Your's is wrong and ONLY mine is right?" I think it a terrible thing when religious people do each other this way. Correction is one thing but dictating just how God is going to reveal Himself to us is another. I was living in Atwood Oklahoma with my grandfather and his third maybe forth wife and her two children. I attended the First Baptist church because most of my family was in fact baptist.

I received my very first bible while there, it was my birthday and my step-mom handed me a $20 bill and dropped me off at a store to buy my own bible.

What a way to remember a birthday. Despite the continuous negative atmosphere, I attended church, I participate and I ended up at Falls Creek Camp for the summer. This would be my very first spiritual experience. I had a lot of questions, questions that should have been answered by parents or a preacher yet they were now being answered by peers.

Sound Familiar?
stop being a little boy to be a child of God?

What about dating and girls?
  What about kissing and hugging?
    What about my dreams and thoughts?
      And what about M_____n?

Is all this stuff wrong? In short, do I have to stop being a BOY to be a Child of God? NO!
I accepted the Lord as my Saviour at Falls Creek in Oklahoma as did many other teen-aged kids. But just how many of us knew exactly what we were doing and why. More important, how many are now lost because they simply did not understand? Certainly, within a few short weeks I was baptized by water and saw a small change in myself but no real conversation experience. Never once was I encouraged to "feed my spirit" or " to become strong in spirit.

Slowly, I returned to my old childish ways and my old fleshly habits. The new man that had been birthed at Falls Creek was slowly dying to his old earthly ways once again. The Spirit Man was dying from starvation. All the urging by the Holy Spirit could not defeat the will of man. At times I would pray or read thus feeding my dying spirit a little. However, monthly and weekly feedings are never enough to build a strong spirit. Like our bodies, our spirit MUST be fed daily (3 or 4 time) to have a chance to grow strong. Before long I forgot about my rebirth, I ignored my spirit and I allowed the Old Rebellious Self to grow stronger. Although "saved" by authority of the Bible I was headed through " the wide gate " very quickly. I became less of a Servant and more self-serving. I produced no fruit and unknowing to me added nothing to my heavenly account. I did not care about bring glory to anyone but myself and certainly not an unseen God. In short, I had deemed Jesus' death meaningless which makes God cry. And because of my actionsHe is going to cry for quite awhile.

All the water in the world, all the prayers in the world cannot always help those who refuse to help themselves. You see, God gave us this thing called free will, No, not Free Willy, but free will. And no matter that, no matter how much He loves us,

He will NOT interfere with OUR FREE WILL!

"I know the plans I have for you"...........
He even knows the hairs on our head!

CHAPTER FOUR

The High school years were tough! My alcohol and drug addiction spiraled out of control as did my sexual antics. Occasional use and sin became a daily grind of use and be used. No longer could I claim to be a Weekend Warrior, I was a full blown Addict in many forms. My own spiritual life all but died yet I maintained a few relationships that kept me partially plugged in. Usually nothing I did, but the religious attempts of those people who tried to love me. My best friend at the time, Roger Pearce believed in Jesus and we talked about Him some. Jesus tried hard to get him and I closer but I had other ideas and today feel like I was a drain on Roger. He seldom cussed, never lied and I felt our drinking was NOT ok with him much of the time. Although my best friend of the era, we did not stay that way long. We each went our different ways.

Roger's mother Delpha was great too. A very Christian

lady who prayed for us often and may still till this day. She went to church every Sunday and prayed for all the men of her life. She was/is such a Godly woman and I know that it was her prayers that has brought me to where I am today. She always invited me to church along with Roger but I do not remember ever accepting. I am sure Roger did from time to time but neither of us enough to feed our ever ailing spirits. You know, I actually should not be talking for Roger so just strike that last little bit, ok. I would never do anything to hurt him or the entire Pearce Family. Most people understand how it was and who I was. Especially, the Pearce and the Hammonds Family.

Gary and Charlotte Hammonds, like Ken and Delpha Pearce, prayed for me often and witnessed to me every chance they got. These four people are my oldest living friends, a fact that I am both proud and ashamed of. I have not done relationships very well. Not God, not Jesus and certainly not the important people of my life. I only wished I had judged myself AS LIITLE as these fine people had. I only wish I had forgiven myself as quickly as they did, maybe, just maybe I could have understood the love of God sooner.

Surely, as my habits got worse, God heard the prayers of these righteous people and answered them by keeping me alive. My own family, although nowhere near as bad as I had their own faults and problems. Most, like me,struggled with church and their idea of being Christian. No, I am not judging it is not my place to judge, I am simply stating the facts as they affected my life in Christ. I am certain they loved me and cared for me, possibly even prayed for me, yet I am unsure how God received their prayers? Maybe I am wrong or mistaken about "another's" spiritual life but one views life through the fruit of their labor. No fruit, no labor, sorry. Forgive me for this negative comparison, I am only trying to be honest and not at the expense of others.God hears all prayers but He answers them according to His will and favor. Much of the time we are praying the wrong prayer or asking in the wrong season. There must be a purity and a sincerity in our hearts for God to answer our prayers. My other friends, my drug buddies and my various sexual encounters talked of prayer, we even spoke of the spiritual life BUT we never actually done anything about it. Our spirits were so far gone I could not remember the last time I felt it. I could be wrong but other than Gary and Delpha, I do not recall any of my so-called friends talk of God or Jesus. The short visits, the chance meeting prepared by God were the only times Jesus was mentioned. Although Gary and I remain somewhat close I still feel I have failed in many of relationships that should matter. People that cared, people that prayed are no more a thought than those I used drugs with. I really should be more grateful and that gratitude should show through a strong Christian relationship. I know this precept to be true in our relationship with Jesus and I'll bet it's true in ALL relationships. Prove me wrong!

CHAPTER FIVE

Struggling with commitment, struggling with addiction, my moral fiber eroded leaving a huge gapping hole. With no spiritual advise, with a dying spiritual man, I was at the edge and willing to jump off head first. Criminal acts were no longer a problem and jail time was the norm. While housed in county jail, I met a chaplain that I could relate too. Of course it was a woman and she was quite pretty yet she sparked areas of my spirit that had been dead or dying for a long time. During one of our lengthy conversations I explained just how I felt. I went on the say that I was like a man walking on a muddy road. One foot seemed to always be on hard road and the other always seem to be dragged in the mud. The example held true for walking down a railroad track as a young boy. We would walk with one foot on the track and one foot off. Sooner or later our "timing" would fail us and we would fall usually skinning or knees or elbows. She would explain scripture and how my example really expressed a criminal's life. She said I should meditate on this and let God reveal to me what it all really meant. I tried real hard but meditation was was not one of my assets. I was so consumed with self, my world revolved so fast that stopping my mind seemed impossible. My good friend Chris Terry said once " you cannot make your brain stop, you have to let it stop." Of course, I did not understand that either but I "thought" about it a lot. I simply could not find a way to stop my spinning brain. In jail, headed to prison, the whole idea of a spiritual life eluded me. I had to be tough! I could not show weakness!

And I surely could not let my brain stop for one second or something might happen, right? How could I ignore what my brain was doing long enough to hear God's " small still voice " whispering to me?

Once in prison I attended church but usually just to get out of my cell. Or there were the occasions where they had cookies or ice cream and I went for that. I do not remember attending church to feed my spirit but then again I am not God. so who knows? Several times I went to a men's bible study before work. I was accused of being "weak" or " having jail-house conversion" so I usually only went once or twice.

My usual question was how could God forgive me when I have sinned so much? Or, I believe my score card is full, heaven may not be an option, ok. Stopping sin is as hard as stopping mu brain. I could not stop my brain to meditate and I could not stop my flesh from sinning. That's all there was! I am pretty much an OCD, I cannot stop my brain from doing what it does. I cannot possibly stop my stinking thinking as the treatment folks put it. It just not humanly possible- Thats Right- It's NOT humanly possible, ALONE!

Left to my own choices I will Self-destruct. Left to my own ideas and attitudes I will commit suicide on the "time payment plan" one drink , one drug , one sex act at a time until my soul is dead. I must put aside my personal ideas and begin a relationship with Jesus Christ. Then I can accept an invitation from the Holy Spirit to be "born again".

Only with the power of the Holy Spirit can I change! Only with some sort of spiritual awakening will I survive! And ONLY with the the Holy Spirit will I find the plan God has for my life.

CHAPTER SIX

Of course, a trip to prison and the parole that followed was NOT that spiritual awakening. Sorry, not yet. I would have to suffer much more before my pain would force a change in my life. My addictions continued to escalate. My destructive behavior ate at my soul and killing my spirit. I was lost in a world of sin and could not find my way out. I surrounded myself with people who validated my habits in some form. Some participated,some agreed while others simply had no judgment at all. For those that suggested recovery or God I avoided at all cost. I wouldn't want to seem ungrateful to those who helped me financially and even mentally. James Meek,Curtis Washington and others are among those. They were good friends,they accepted me and they helped me financially whenever my addictions grew. Places to sleep, cars to drive and money to spend are good things for this world yet they are useless if your soul is dying. I had survived homelessness five, six times, unemployment more than that. It was in these times that God had cared for me,although I did not want it. I soon figured out that God does not love because I am good. I could never live up to Gods own righteousness, it is impossible. God always loved me because HE was good! What I had to do is stop trying and accept his goodness. Although a glimpse of this had formed in my mind,the entire picture,the whole expression of Gods love would take another decade.

I would have to change several "Other" God ideas before a full baptism of His grace would take hold. I would first have to find sobriety,then I would need Steve B and Dan Childs to add to the prayers of Gary Hammond. I had walls that must be torn down. I was confused about religion verses spiritually. I could not understand Grace under my current circumstances. I needed a Spiritual Experience. I needed a Spiritual Awakening. I needed a Rebirth. I had to be born again!

BORN AGAIN...exactly what did that mean and how does it happen? Lord only knows just how confused I was and here I was headed. Born again, why me, why now, didn't He know I just wanted to be high one more time. Just one more run, just one more weekend of raw unadulterated bunny rabbit sex, ok.

CHAPTER SEVEN

Sometime on (or near) November 11,1991.I was born again. I sincerely believe that this is the exact re-birth Jesus Christ spoke of. On that day I accepted the help of Narcotics Anonymous. At the encouragement of Don Jones and his family I walked into my first N.A. meeting in West Fort Worth. Little did I know, I was at home and so much closer to the Love of God. This was my second Spiritual Awakening - 11\11\91. As comical and controversial as they may be, the 12 steps as written for A.A. and N.A. were the key to this spiritual awakening. I needed something simplistic,I needed an elementary guide to God's grace. My previous "Religious Experiences" had been detrimental to my spiritual growth. Possibly, it was Satan using my own faults to confuse me, but I lean toward the religious elitism that Jesus spoke of as the true problem. The 12 steps put aside religious bias and elitism and grabbed a hold of basic spiritual principals. This is what I needed. This is what the entire world needs. Each addict, each alcoholic,each porn dependent person must have a spiritual experience to change. Otherwise,like me, they will continue to destroy their lives one habit, one sin at a time. Some consider the "God of your understanding" concept as wrong. Some think it blaspheming to not condemn others for NOT believing in Jesus. Yet it is Jesus who taught of the "faith of a mustard seed". Isn't a belief in any God for now just that, a faith of a mustard seed? It does not take a very big crack for the Holy Spirit to step in and start doing His work. It does not take much a step toward God for Him to start moving toward us.

Willingness to believe, no matter how small is a start folks! Many times all a person must do is seek God or express a desire to seek God and God usually does much more. Instead so many stand confused about religious doctrine or unfounded rituals that even Jesus warned us about. I simply accept the chance that there was a God and that I was not it. I accept that I had tried everything else and nothing changed. I accepted that with my own choices I had destroyed my life. Then,I surrendered to God as best I could at that time & that place!

That was all the crack my wall needed. That was the chink in my armor that God needed. And He then manifested Himself inside of me and I began to grow. Was I healed? NO! Was I Sinless? NO! Was I Born Again? YES! the truth, if you have faith as small as a **mustard seed**, you can say to this mountain, 'Move through that one man, how much **more** will those who receive God's **abundant** provision of grace and of the gift of righteousness reign in **life** through the one man, Jesus Christ.**search**es all things, even the deep things of God

CHAPTER EIGHT

Dan Childs and I struggled just about the same. We both had a loving concept of God but struggled with in ourselves with the idea of Jesus. We found it hard to understand how a " Loving God" who saved us would not save others based on the idea of "The Jesus Plan" ? As sad as it may sound, no religious person we found could fully explain this aspect of God's Love as expressed in the books of the New Testament. Plus our late night conversations about the hypocrites or hypocrisy of most in the religious realm was based on what we had both actually seen and thus right in our face. Still, as so many others, we were searching - endlessly! We held fast on the belief that God would eventually reward our search. We knew from experience that it would be in HIS time, in HIS way. The Bible says at some point that the gifts of the spirit are life and peace. In another verse(I can't seem to find today) the Bible says "and life more abundantly". Dan and I were experiencing just that each day.

Unintentionally, we began to separate ourselves from the more agnostic people. Dan and I experiment with several churched as we were gently urged by the Holy Spirit. A separation due to personal reasons introduced me to Steve B. Steve was a believer in Jesus Christ and had a question he asked at my discomfort " how are you and Jesus getting along today?" were usually the first words Steve would ask. His other favorite which grated on my nerves was "what have you learned today?" Of course, he was looking for one of these "God is good", "Jesus is king",or "He has risen". My usual reply was a short "nothing".

My relation with Jesus was nothing and I felt I knew nothing. Steve, unlike Dan, was set in his Jesus belief so he seldom debated religion. He cared very little for religious rules or elitism and stood firm on "the Jesus deal". Steve and I were sitting in a Whataburger,(I believe).An employee of Whataburger, Rose, over heard us talking and ask me a single question "Sir, what if your wrong?" Excuse me... "I'm just asking, what if your wrong about Jesus?" Well then I'm wrong! "But what have you got to lose" The words would haunt me for several days. During that time I would have my third spiritual awakening. I have accepted the love of Jesus!

CHAPTER NINE

Now , I had an answer for Steve's question " I'm searching for Jesus." I began to open up more to the entire idea that Jesus was the way to live. I attended church with Gary Hammonds, I attended church with Dan Childs. And I accepted each invitation to church that came along. As well, I ask others about their church. I inquired about what they looked for in a church? How can anyone attend a church they disagree with? Finally, some years later,I accepted Steve's invitation! I was married to my current wife Linda, my third and last OK! She had told me about a prayer (she had) for a man that would attend church with her. I explained my new found beliefs and told her of Steve's invitation. As life would have it... she went long before I did due to an assignment in Kentucky. However, God did fulfill her prayer. One day soon, I sat with her in University Park Church and I heard the great preacher Jeff Wickwire. I was amazed at the feeling, the the emotion, so much, that I simply sat and weeped. The walls of shame and pain began to fall. The built up anger at God flowed with each tear. I had began a healing process between God and I. Actually, it may have been a healing between Myself and I! This was my forth spiritual awakening! Actually thanks to pastor Jeff Wickwire there were a series of events that cover six weeks that became my forth (& fifth) spiritual awakening. He was preaching on Hebrews 6:1-3.The cornerstone of the Christian faith. I happened to be there each Sunday. Each Sunday, six in all, a miracle happened specify to me before, during and after

Pastor Jeff's service. The first had to do with a lighted meter that hung on the wall of the sanctuary and counted the weekly tithe. That lighted meter validated how I felt about money. It bothered me. The week his six part sermon started, Pastor Jeff walked in and announced that God had revealed to him that the meter was offensive so he had it removed. I had not said a word to anyone! Next Sunday I had understood all about two baptisms. I believe it was the third or forth Sunday that the church had a drawing. For some reason, I was very angry that day. Possibly, I had to leave for work or something.

Anyway, my wife Linda put my name in the drawing. The entire service I prayed for God to "prove" himself to me by allowing me to win. Of course, I had no faith in the challenge. YET ... I WON!! Hebrews 6 also says that we will move on to maturity " If God permits." Finally God had permitted me to move to another level. One more awakening, one more vision, one more step closer to God. Wow , what a God we have. And what a servant Pastor Jeff is, never failing, never faltering just one step after another toward eternity and heaven.

28

CHAPTER TEN

One would hope that great changes would happen? Sorry, but only a few small changes took place!

Most changes come in accordance with our pain. Once our pain is great enough we become willing to accept God's way, not our own. This held true for me. With plenty of tools, with tons of knowledge, and with loads of personal support, I still refused to accept the love and forgiveness of my Lord and savior Jesus Christ? And God was still good to me! Why did I rebel so much, why do we "kick against the pricks"? And why volunteer for even more pain? Two trips to North Carolina, two more excellent churches and still I cried to be home. A trip to Virginia and one to Longview Texas, yet I moaned in pain at the travels I had to endure. Why did I volunteer for this misery? Why did I need these jobs away from home? Or ...A) was it the job at all? B) was it the money? C) was it simply me? Soon, I found out, soon I realized God's true intentions. Soon, it all became so clear. Soon, I had a sixth spiritual awakening.

And it happened, yes, at University Park Church, although Pastor Jeff was no longer there. A missionary was there from China, India, somewhere. He explained (unlike others) how hard it is to be a missionary and that " our purpose is where ever our pay check is." Our mission, our purpose is exactly where we are TODAY! Change of job, change of residence is not always needed to achieve our purpose. It all made sense! It was exactly what I needed to hear.

Where ever I went, Whatever city I visited, that was exactly where God wanted me that day. Suddenly, in a split second, I understood I had a spiritual awakening # 6. This man never knew me and I never him. My wife didn't know, nor did Steve. No one but God & I understood until I began to share it in my story or testimony. This was yet another bonifide miracle supplied by Jesus Christ through University Park Church. What an anointing, what a blessing, this humble church has been to me, to my family and to many of my friends. My life began to change quicker than ever before once I spent much of my waking hours looking for my next mission, **my next single day's purpose.**

CHAPTER ELEVEN

Some would call it a "new pair of glasses",others may say a "para dime shift."While others would stick with "purpose" or "calling." I'll stay with a spiritual awakening. Unless a person has a true spiritual awakening change is impossible. Alcoholics struggle, addicts die and the depressed continue to medicate at a rate of $20 billion per year. Each of theseare curable with a personal spiritual awakening. The 12 steps, Celebrate Recovery and other Cornerstone type programs are a map to having a spiritual awakening. For me it lead to more than one! And any of you can do the same, you too can have a spiritual awakening that leads to a great change. And that change eventually leads us all back to God. For me, I was off to Wichita Falls, where I attended church at Church of the Living Water. Pastors Tim and Pam were great. They welcomed me and my wife with open arms. I reached out, helping people to understand addiction coupled with other problems. I spoke on several radio stations while writing many letters to the editor for local papers. I grew BOLDLY in Christ. I had a smile on my face and Jesus in my heart, and I suppose people could see that? I made friends, encouraged folks and was of service where ever possible. I put no restriction on what, who or where! Oh, I hit stumbling blocks. Hastings books has been "a thorn in my side" everywhere I go.

They simply cannot tell the truth. But, I refused to, lower myself to their level. I was kind and considerate each time. Some of our state's newspapers are the same. They avoid a Christian conservative at all cost. And why, we are the majority! God wants me to grow a good

Christian character and these people are provided by God to do just that. God wants me to have manors, integrity and the Fruits of the Spirit. He provides me with people from Hastings and Book-a-Million to exercise those fruits and manors. God has a plan for our lives and it does not include anger, rage or violence. He wants us to be useful and that will not happen if we are rude or inconsiderate. God's people reflect God's image-- that's how people know us!

CHAPTER TWELVE

Maybe my most rewarding trip has been to Vega Texas. This is, in part, due to the people of Vega combined with the growth God has given me. I contributed very little in the entire process, other than, accepting God's plan for being there. One of my habits as I enter new towns, is to attend church at one of the Methodist churches then ask about another non-denomination in town. Basically, I have found that Methodist are more than willing to help you however they can. Few ever try to push their beliefs onto those who are looking elsewhere. In Vega, God had other ideas. While sitting in the cafe I overheard two men talking. One happen to be the   pastor Christ Community Fellowship,Mr. Craig Solomon. We spoke and I was invited to attend church on Sunday. I did and I never looked anywhere else. The people of Christ Community Fellowship were the living embodiment of Christ. They were full of love, compassion and service. I was amazed at what I witnessed and it helped to bring out the best in me. Maybe it is small town America, maybe it's the farm and ranch mentality that is so dependent on God? I have no answers, just knowledge that it's there. As my own trust grew I began to participate more and more. I wrote a monthly column for the church newsletter. I was honored with several OP/ED'S in the local paper. And I spoke on drugs and alcohol a dozen times. All the while, I made friends with literally hundreds of wonderful folks.

At one low spot, I was speaking with Pastor Craig and he spoke of "going through deliverance". We talked about it several times, and on one Sunday we did just that. He(God), deliveredme from my family curses and my generational burdens. I offered forgiveness and I received forgiveness. This was not a spiritual awakening like the others; it was more like a spiritual healing but a spiritual awakening none the less. There was really no change, no real growth, just acceptance of forgiveness and belief in what God does. Shortly after this I went on possibly the most remarkable weekend of my life. Pastor Craig sponsored me and I went to the Walk to Emmaus. WOW! If ever I had needed a burning bush, if ever I desired the face of God, I saw it that weekend. I witnessed the love of God and had my seventh spiritual awakening in 49 years. I can never thank the people of Christ Community Fellowship and Golden Spread Emmaus enough for my weekend!

Heck, I have lost count? Isn't this Awakening 8 & 9? Wow, I would have to look back and see. I had sort of put these two and two others all in one catagory! Isn't God good?

May God continuously Bless you ALL

CHAPTER THIRTEEN

Too suggest that there is only one way to have a spiritual experience is false. Too claim that one must be religious to have a spiritual awakening is simply untrue. The AA and NA books on the 12 steps talk very specifically about spiritual awakenings an experience

Hundreds of people each year have spiritual experiences through literally hundreds of these recovery type programs. In the bible, Jesus refers to sheep, which is plural, as well as flocks which is also plural. Can there be only one religion or only one way to our Lord Jesus Christ? I doubt it! Yet thousands of religious elitist claim just that each Sunday. By doing that, they do what Jesus never did, exclude the sick, poor and uneducated. We are God's children too, there are no step-children or any half children. "We can all beGod's children". Jesus seldom stayed in a church or a temple. When he did, he usually got mad. Jesus seldom, if ever, performed a miracle in church. His place was with the people - ALL people! Where can anyone gain anything else from all that He said?

God is NOT in a church! Just read it yourself!

Rather factually, when Jesus was angry, He was usually angry with religious leaders and not with you or I. When He spoke of hypocrites and fools, He was not talking to us , as so many religious folks would have you believe. He was in fact, talking to THEM, the clicks, the religious elites who build walls around themselves and the average person. He loves us so much that He gave His life for us. He loved us so much that He pointed out over and over again the faults of the religious leadership and much of it fits just as well today. We and they were doomed to the pits of Hell and then He (not them) gave us a way out. Jesus wants to be surrounded by average people for eternity. Most of us cannot begin to understand this kind of love. In our society we view the rich and powerful as something desirable, Jesus does not. In our society the sick and poor are some thing to escape from, not for Jesus. Jesus looks at our hearts and He views us through our desired actions not through a bank account or trust fund. Few of us have anything to compare to the rich, yet few of them have anything to compare to a life with Jesus Christ.

Broken families, Broken Homes and Broken Vows, both share the pains of human life but few will share in the eternity of Heaven. Strangled by rules and regulations, taxed to poverty by an exceedingly larger government, so many of us lose hope and turn away from any sort of religious affiliation or political grouping. We then turn away from God and family.

Not Me!

With the compassion of my wife Linda, with the help of my friends Steve and Tricia B. I learned how to put these worldly things aside and lean solely on my relationship with Jesus Christ. And with that my vision of unconditional love began to change and I began to sort out exactly who I cared about and who I did not. I began to weep at Easter! I saw Christmas through different eyes and then one day I woke up with a new idea of just how God wanted me to live. Oh, no, I was not delivered! Nor did I grow fruit over night. I still had my struggles but at least I knew how God would like me to live to love; not boast, or be proud.

---

that whoever believes in him shall not perish but have eternal life.

---

unfailing love surrounds the man who trusts in him.

CHAPTER FOURTEEN

Please do not think or believe that I despise all spiritual leaders, preachers or even televangelist. I happen to have some very strong opinions about the way some things are going here in America and around the world. I do not hate anybody; matter of fact the Bible says these people will be held to a higher standard of judgment and I am content letting God do that. However, like it or not many of these people, with all the good they may have done, have led many people to turn their backs on church and Jesus Christ. By setting the records straight, by doing what Jesus has called me to do, maybe many of these lost people can once again find truth and freedom in the walls of a church. I consider my own opinion an asset to those confusedor lost. I aim to do my very best to help as many people as possible find Jesus Christ. I am, like some of my words imply - Building Bridges that others have destroyed. Some want to pick and chose the scripture they use to shame and guilt folks into tithing.

Many want to avoid scriptures on love and grace all together as a way to avoid being labeled a "feel good church". What's wrong with feeling good? What's wrong with true Christian freedom?

Weeks of preaching on the "End of Times", thousands of lessons on tithing and even more on The Law when in fact we are not under Law we are under Grace. Why not preach on the Meaninglessness of higher education and books from Ecclesiastes? Why not preach on avoiding worry from Matthew?

With mega-churches popping up in every city one cannot help but believe that it is a marketing plan laid out by some huge non-profit - profit building corporation. Yes, there are just those kind of people - people who show non-profit entities just how to make non-profit profit. Sound confusing - it is! Bill boards, commercials and advertising is all part of some churches success. The average Joe, myself included struggle with the spiritual implications of this type of church. We simply do not understand nor can we justify it through scripture. Does that mean it is wrong - No - just that the average America is skeptical of a preacher making *a million dollars per year in salary?*

Wow, did I chase some rabbits on this one. I am so sorry that I went of the deep end on this subject. Not that I intend to change one word, however, I did not mean to spend so much time on the subject. "God does for us what we cannot do for ourselves" If we could save ourselves than we would not need Him or church. Of course as always this is just my opinion and my personal ideas based on my experience. It does not make it fact for you. You may have totally different ideas about how churches are formed and just how they are marketed, I always thought it was suppose to be Jesus who received all the GLORY?

My concern is not the plate or the tithe amount, my concern is the souls and salvation of those who happen to walk away from a misunderstanding or argument. My concern is the souls of addicts and alcoholic who struggle with the elitism and clicks of so many large churches.

The rich, the over-educated and the spiritual leaders have much more of an opportunity than the less fortunate. Jesus set the mark and used all the proper examples yet today we still see the same exclusion among many who refuse to accept the convicted felon or thief as a child of God. It is my sincere and honest belief that Jesus' own life bares witness to how we should be treating those less fortunate. And Yes there are some who follow the example of Jesus and there are others who resemble the Jewish Leadership, separating themselves from everyone on the basis of being "unclean" or "unworthy".

We must check and double check the writings to the many churches by Paul. His instructions, his experience holds true today as much as ever. Many have distorted the lines and lives of Paul into things unbelievable by many. We must return to the simple basics and stop trying to tell the future through scriptural interpretation. We must re-visit the Red Letters and meditate fully on those before moving on to scripture we cannot possibly understand. We must concern ourselves with **"board is the way and wide is the gate that leads to destruction" Yet "narrow is the way and narrow is that gate that leads to salvation".**

Why do we never hear a mega-church preach this?

Do you think their marketing plan would fall apart if they stopped preaching "prosperity"? I know, I know, I said I would stop and I will. This piece is suppose to be light hearted and informational and I pray that it is. I am sorry if, unlike Ben Franklin and others, I have opinions that I simply cannot NOT share. Ben became such a good example of elder-statesmanship. He was a humble man in that latter years and able to refrain from sharing opinions that might offend. I am not there- YET!

To explain one's spiritual experience, I believe one must provide the obstacles and stumbling blocks that one went through. I have done that to the best of my ability.

Too many that I have ministered too have tried religion only to be left empty and alone by the aftermath of elitism. To many need the fellowship of the church but continuously compare their "outsides" to other's "insides".

I have witnessed churches where the pastor was protected by security and no one was able to counsel with him. I have seen mega0churches where the preachers or pastor was behind 3-4 even 5 locked doors. Where can anyone validate these measures in the Bible or **the life of Jesus Christ?**

CHAPTER FIFTEEN

Those that I seek are those that try to fill that hole deep inside(gut) with drugs, alcohol, sex or money. Those that I try and minister to are empty and dying inside because of one bad habit or another. Those I seek to help are the poor, the down cast, the pit bull and the parolee who all seem to find no place in the country we claim is free. I seek to inform them that by having a spiritual awakening, by having no place in this world MIGHT actually secure them a place in eternity if they would only seek a relationship with Jesus Christ. If, I can ONLY get them to accept Jesus Christ on His word then their circumstance in this world just simply would not matter. The meek, the humble, the poor and the impoverished are exactly the people Jesus preached to and they are the same people I want to preach to. Where can the modern church view any other idea of Christianity than in this manor?

Of course we have those who claim prophesy and visions. I would never be the one to deny those. Yet Jesus Himself warned of False Prophets. As well we are warned of false teachers and a false word or deception that will be sent. I actually had this feeling about Rick's "Purpose Driven Church". I had dreamed that it was just that - a great deception sent to fool the non-believers. Today, I am still skeptical but having heard Rick preach and been to his church, I have changed my mind a little. He is a good man but more important, " a kingdom divided cannot stand". In truth, I would much rather heed the warning and find my own way with the support of a few than to be deceived and fall into the pits of hell by following the many. This way my eyes and ears are opened by God and I find my way because of God, and I know for sure when God has revealed His word to me. This is my prayer for every one of you - that you too be NOT deceived by false teachers and that you hear the word as it is presented by God to you through a trustedservant. Is this book it - I think so! Is my way the only way - I think so! Yet at the same time, I would never tell you or anyone else that they are WRONG! As always, I simply tell you what I believe and you can then make your own choices based on a different set of opinions.

Matthew 24:5

For many shall come in my name, saying, I AM CHRIST; AND SHALL DECEIVE MANY

---

certain men not to teach **false** doctrines any longer

———————

just as there will be **false teachers** among you. They will secretly introduce destructive heresies

———————

speak truthfully to his neighbor, for we are all members of one body.

———————

but whoever is not from God does not listen to us. This is how we recognize the Spirit of truth and the spirit of **falsehood**.

CHAPTER SIXTEEN

Ok, fine, enough is enough. I have said just about all I want to say about all that. I know, I have said that for three chapters only to refuse to move on.   So instead on continuing on this same subject and loosing some of you I will try my best to return my focus to the Variety of the Spiritual Awakening and just how we are born again in the Spirit. To do that I must discuss religion some. And I must be able to accept other people's personal beliefs. Am I being repetitious, urely not?   What I am saying is that through my spiritual awakenings I must be strong enough in my own beliefs to allow other people theirs. I do not need to waste time telling others they are wrong. Simply state my own beliefs and let God do the rest. If I cannot find some sort of acceptance in another's beliefs then I can certainly never be happy. And if I cannot find open mindedness within myself then I doubt I will ever see anyone else as open minded. I will assume that everyone is as closed minded as I. In fact, as with many 12 step programs , open minded and willing along with a great amount of acceptance are the keys to recovery, any type of recover.

So with some 6 million people suffering from addiction, with another 6 million on probation or parole, I can say that this is my church, these are my people. 12 million people, some lost souls, some separated from the Father all because of some spiritual misunderstanding. Wow, and to think that so many want nothing to do with

"THOSE PEOPLE". I did not think I needed a building, I do not believe I need a stadium or Colosseum, yet if God wants me to have one to house these people as they walk their journey then I shall do it with the faith and prayer of George Muller, George Whitefield and Jeff Wickwire. I will do it through the Holy Spirit and an additional spiritual awakening to the ideas and attitudes of Jesus Christ and Paul.With God in charge I try to write these books, I speak, I preach and I teach to those who will listen. Nothing is hidden in the Bible nor is it left to those higher educated than I, the bible tells me so. The followers of Jesus, Jesus Himself and many others were simple, uneducated people with an anointing. An anointing of the Holy Spirit or spiritual awakening through the knowledge of the bible. Jesus died for all of us who are called. God gave the bible to everyone who would read it. It is the Holy Spirit that reveals God's word to us not man and it is the Holy Spirit that determines a person's spiritual awakening. Yes, God may use others as He used Steve B and Pastor Jeff with me. And with each spiritual awakening God used someone filled with the Holy Spirit to bring me the anointing He wanted me to have. Once we are baptized with the Holy

Spirit many of the Bible's so-called secrets are then revealed to us on a one-on -one basis. "Let those with ears , hear." As much as we need accountability, as much as we desire true maturity, we witness that a spiritual experience, an awakening of the spirit must come first before many of God's questions can be answered.

Only then did I see what was most important and what never needed argued over. Hebrews 6:1-2-3 and the " Finding the Rock " bible study lead by Pastor Jeff quiet possibly was the most important few days I ever spent in church.

Finding maturity, being led on to perfection and knowing God's plan for us has very little to do with education, and everything to do with an open door or willingness and faith. God wants us , to want too, have a relationship with the one person able to save us - Jesus Christ. God wants us to see just how futile our human experiences are and what could happen if we awaken to the full power of the Holy Spirit. He wants us to slow down long enough to gain just enough knowledge to fully awaken spiritually, then accept the full knowledge of His Word -

The Holy Bible!

It is not about a building - it is about a relationshipIt is not about a language - it is about a relationship It is not about which bible is right - it is about a relationship. It is not about a dress or a tie - it is about a relationship

A relationship with the ONLY person to ever claim exactly what Jesus claimed - I died as a sacrifice for YOU!

PART TWO

Wash your hands, you sinners, and purify your hearts, you **double-minded**.

Over the last 30 plus pages I have given you just that - My opinion. Some ore pretty bold while others may be considered harsh. I am sorry, as I have stated, these are things revealed to me by the word of God and not man.

I have a great respect for the many men and women of God but meeting once a year at conventions across this nation to decide what the rest of us are going to believe this next year is wrong. God never changes and His word never changed . Why then would so many **over-educated -under- fed- leaders** need to search out ways to discredit another's faith? Next is the idea of knowing exactly who we are in Christ. Who is the man in the mirror? Looking at the scriptures listed above we see just how important knowing who we are is.

Jesus wants us to be BOLD for Him. He wants us HOT - not lukewarm.

So with that thought in mind we must know our values, our beliefs and our morals. Not some relative idea or grey-matter thinking but ABSOLUTELY WHO WE ARE!

For many shall come in my name, saying, I am Christ; and shall deceive many.

(Matthew 24:5)

Remembering How God Made Us - **Victorious**

I remember some years ago, I was at a prison ministry convention called " Bridging the Gap. You may have heard me use that term some these days. There I walked up to a table for The Federal Prison. I read a little then the guy ask - " Are you interested" I said "yes but I am sorry I do not qualify." He smiled, actually sort of laughed and said " Why not just fill out the form and let God do the rest." Well.... the form was 10 pages long and if I did not qualify why on God green Earth would I waste my time? God was calling me then...

"They were miners, they were 100% illiterate, stuck in degradation that defies words. George Whitefield walked among them in full Lutheran garb, preaching Matthew 5 " Blessed are the poor in spirit for theirs is the Kingdom of Heaven. Whitfield wrote later in his diary " the white gutters made by their tears ran down their black cheeks...."Whitfield heard God call and he listen, What do we do when we hear God's call? Whitefield no longer could find a place to preach. Even his attempt at going into the local prison was stopped by religious authority."

The Bible gives us specific examples of just how God is going to call. All we have to do is read it and we see how to answer:

Exodus 3:11 Moses told Lord : Who am I to go to Pharaoh or bring the Israelites out?

Judges 6:15 Gideon told Lord: My clan is the weakest and I am the weakest of my clan

John 6:9 Andrew told Lord; Here is a boy with 5 loaves & 2 fish but how far will that go

1 Samuel 17 32-34 David said -Let no one lose heart on account of this Philistine, your servant will go and fight him

Luke 1:38 the 17 year old Mary said I am the Lord's servant ; May it be to me as You have said, Lord

The great writer and philosopher Edmund Burk said it rightly - " all that is necessary for the triumph of EVIL is that good men do NOTHING.

Jesus said - " I know thy works thou are neither cold or hot. Thou art lukewarm." And of course who can deny the intent of the Parable of the Talents; we have all been given a share of something to use. We all have a gift God has given us to bring glory to Him by helping other people.

God has a call on your life – Have you answered YET.

THE ELEMENTARY TEACHINGS
OF JESUS CHRIST

Hebrews 6:1-3

Repentance from acts that lead to death(sin) 1 John 1:9,
Matt. 4: 12-17, Luke 18:9-14, Acts 2:38-41

Faith In God – Matthew 6:25-34, Romans 3:21 &5:11
Hebrews 11

_____

_____

Baptism(S)- Matthew 3:1-12, & 28:16, Romans 6:1-5 Acts 10:47, Acts 15:8 (2nd Baptism)

_____

_____

_____

Laying on of Hands – Acts 8:15-19, Acts 9:17-18, Acts 13:2, Matthew 8:3 & 9:18-26

_____

_____

_____

Resurrection of the Dead – Matt.27:57, 1 Cor. 15, Acts 1:1

_____

_____

_____

Eternal Judgment- Isa. 66:16, Matt. 12:36, 2Cor. 5:10-12

_____

_____

_____

And God Permitting, we will do so" Hebrews 6:3NIV

These are the elementary teaching of our Lord Jesus Christ, it says so.Do you realize the importance of understanding them? We must use the scriptures provided to gain wisdom and insight into what Jesus wants us to know and learn.

One of the greats, Rick, Jeff , or maybe even TD said"If you know how to Worry, then you know how to meditate." Worry is thinking about future events that are usually negative. Meditation is worrying about positive events as they pertain to God. Stop worrying about things you cannot possibly predict and start focusing on God's plan and His Promises. It all beginswith Hebrews 6:1-3 and understanding God's Teachings.

Your Thoughts _____

_____

_____

_____

_____

_____

VALUES AND BELIEFS
PART ONE

If I forget my past then
I forget my mistakes ....

If I forget my mistakes then
I forget what I need to learn......

If I forget what I need to learn then
I must admit I don't know.........

<u>WHO I AM IN GOD!</u>

By examining my beliefs and the value I place on each I begin to learn who I am and what my purpose is. Without this exploration I cannot find the true meaning of life. I can only wonder through life aimlessly without PURPOSE.

Your own thoughts or ideas thus far,

_____

_____

_____

_____

_____

_____

_____

_____

_____

VALUES AND BELIEFS
PART TWO

A human being has a value we place on ourselves

A value that is determined by how we feel about " I "

Most of us do NOT value ourself as we should

If we make a "wish list" it usually falls short.

How much money are you willing to loan ?

How far are you willing to give a ride?
How long can a friend stay on your couch?

How many hours per day do we work?

Each question has an answer,
we never have to think about.

Although we ignore it,
we have an inherent value built in.

This value, this finite amount,
is written on our conscience.

What we must do to increase it,
is search out and know it.

VALUES AND BELIEFS
PART THREE

Why do we make the choices we make?

Why does certain things make us angry?

Why is it that we offer things but then get mad?

Why would God wire us in such a manner?

We get so consumed with Life that we lose US!

We forget who we are, what we believe of Life!
This exercise, will reunite US with Ourselves!

Your raising gave you inherent values.

Some things came from God, most from our parents.

Many need to be changed to fulfill God's Purpose.

A scary thought for those of us who fear change.

Could it be that you really don't want to know truth?

Strange, that we would volunteer for misery and pain?

YOUR IDEAS;_____

_____

_____

QUESTIONS AND DEFINITIONS

Over the last pages you have been asked questions,

Each of these questions have a specific meaning in life.

By answering honestly, you too can grow & prosper.

Now, it's time to define what we believe even further

Define Each Categories

1. Friends
2. Non-Sexual Relations
3. Best Friends

6. Sexual Relations
7. Church Members
8. Social Interactions

| 4. Family Members | 9. Accountability |
| 5. Co-workers | 10. Other |

Define Each Word

1.	Honor	4. Dating or Courting
2.	Respect	5. Charity or Giving
3.	Fun	6. Love

Now let us return to the ideas and attitudes I began with, ok. You can return to this work as time permits or as God places it on your hearts to grow closer to Him through His son Jesus Christ. Remember this is a **Spiritual Journey!** We have now had a **Spiritual Awakening** and the Spirit will lead us on our path or **Spiritual Trip** - **To Our Inheritance as a Child of God!**

CHAPTER SEVENTEEN

Today, early 2007, I am somewhat comfortable in my own skin. I desire but a little, I am seeking to be totally debt free and I create only a few problems associated with sin. Usually, things temperamental or along the lines of anger.I am unsure of the test set before me or the character asset I must develop to be rid of these emotional upheavals but I am aware of them, I am aware of their destructive nature and I know I must change yet again. I have NO DENIAL there. Given my history, I have no doubt that another spiritual awakening of some sort is the change I need to see things differently. We must be re-born each time we must change or we return to the "change by pain syndrome". I remain some what teachable so I must be at least a wee bit humble. I doubt I have any real humility or the amount of humility it takes to be truly happy BUT, I have enough to remain teachable and that equates to change. There is no doubt that I will NEVER know all things about all things.

Those that pretends this premise are too prideful to ever admit they just might be wrong. Those that have $1000'S wrapped up in a meaningless education will never admit they just might have been wrong all along. I accept my journey along with each character flaw. I accept my unknowing right along side my knowing.

I am never too smart to admit I made a mistake. Many of those that came before us chose to "build temples on the fields of victory". I chose to continue on till the ends of the Earth so I might inherit the WHOLE reward. For me none of this is a destination, it is all about today's steps. I conclude that it is the journey, what each man does each day that matters. I try to keep short accounts with God - One Day At A Time Accounts - so that I am fully aware of where I stand on today's journey. If we walk the walk, if we talk the talk, if we take one day at a time, the heavenly destination is part pf God's inherited promise and the roots of our eternal HOPE. With all that said, why do so many attempt "half measures"? Why are so many hiding in church pews across our great nation? And why do so many accept ONLY half the journey.

We are not stupid, lazy maybe but we are all capable of knowing the will of God. Oh, I would change some things in my life but not many. I wish i had not hurt so many people along the way. Today many of the regrets I have are associated with hurt emotions or SHAME!

For some this entire subject may have played out many pages ago. For others it may have just played out. Either way, I am ok with that because I know that God has a plan and I am not in charge of it. You must find your own way, accept your own spiritual journey. We must remain open-minded to all ideas and only then can God speak to us. We must accept assignments we really do not want for God to place the people there we will need to guide us. We must fully understand that we really do not understand. Thus accepting and exercising our one true attribute - FAITH.

Next we need not envy the adventures of others. Envy breeds strife and strife cuts us off from the sunlight of the spirit. Some will receive their rewards here on Earth because they have done their deeds before men. Others will their rewards in Heaven as promised because they did their deeds as part of God's plan. I hope this has helped. I pray that some sort of light has come into your world through these few short words and the Holy Spirit. I know I have received a blessing from writing it and I know that we will meet one day -   on streets paved with gold and lined with heavenly mansions.

Until then my friends if you cannot, (will not) believe then at least would you please believe that I believe until the Holy Spirit blesses you in His own time.

CLOSURE

Who would have believed,
me saying these things to you?

Me and ex-con, recovering drug addict,
once semi-non-believer-agnostic?

Yet, by the grace of God,
I can offer you my experience!

If I can help just one addict recover,

If I can help just 1 parolee not return to prison,

If I can help just 1 person find Jesus Christ,

If I can help 1 person understand the Holy Spirit,

My entire life, my aches & pains,
my misery will not have been in vain,

Your purpose, like mine, is where we are,
right where the check is paid.

We do not have too look far,
God does not make hard work of His Service

ADDENDUM

To believe that I have anything to offer
is sometimes hard for me to envision.

To consider that God may have chosen me
 to do anything is hard to swallow.

To hope that God allow me to help Him
do anything important is humbling.

And yet to accept His anointing and act in
humility and grace is alway hard.

So, that being said, it is very hard for me to even mention
this next part;Prior to finishing this piece I was a simple
construction worker, working for Dunininck Brothers in
Tarrant County. As this piece proceeded, as I wrote more
and more, another story began to unfold. One only God

could have predicted. Today, May 2007, I have been offered a ministry position in the Town of Dumas Texas. This position, if I take it is exactly what I have been dreaming of and praying for years. It would be helping people just like to stay clean and sober. I would be the Executive Director or a Transitional Living Center or Faith-Based Recovery House. Looking back, remembering what has happened to me over the last 3-5 years, I sincerely believe this was where God was leading me all along.

God's plan will be fulfilled.

People like us seem to think we are terminally unique. We believe we are the only ones that feel the way we do and we are always comparing our insides to other people's outsides. Many people look just fine on the outside while they are dying on the inside - this is true for so many addicts. Nationwide, I have found many "saved" religious people hurting badly on the inside. Many continuously hide in church pews and even die trying to look good on the outside. Why?

PRIDE!

The problem is many of us addicts and alcohols wonder into church looking for friendships only to believe exactly what is being presented - a perverted sense of perfectionism. We ALL struggle! It is those struggles and their solutions that mold our character into servants of Jesus Christ. And as we have read, character is one of the things God is looking for. Strangely, it is us, not the religious folk who find recovery first from all our hurts and habits. While 1000s of religious leaders seek to figure out drug addiction and sexual immorality, we addicts can pretty much point them to the chapter and verse - Romans 7:15-20. While they(religious leaders) rewrite doctrine and church rules, while more and more of their congregation die, they chose to ignore the answers from the common folk. This is one selfish act I never understood until now. And now,I have the chance to share with these fine people what is going on that they just cannot seem to figure out.

Thank you God, finally!

The Bible should mold a man's character, the Bible should make men better, yet for decades it's misconception has managed to divide many who seeks it's wisdoms. My desire is to try and change that with the love and grace of Jesus Christ.

From this point on you will be able to read for yourselves what people like I think about religion and religious doctrine. These stories have been combined to help all of us understand each other. God's church, Jesus' church is ONE church. How ever, the words sheep and flocks are plural. So as we present these stories of confusion, confession and contradiction, maybe just maybe God will use this to help everyone understand each other. May God Bless each of you read this and may He walk with you is love and grace through whatever it is you are going through.

PART THREE

PERSONAL STUDIES

Johnette Clark, Dumas Texas

Really God? People with Addictions?

We are really just tired of sitting in the pews. We are into
our own personal relationships, not with YOU but with
others. Others with some big problems! We were just
looking for a ministry. We were just wanting to reach out
but we never imagined it would come in the shape of drug
addiction. We sure did not think we would find him in a
dumpster - HIGH! God had been preparing this church in
this small Texas town for some time. We were growing
spiritually and ready to start sharing when He laid it at our
feet - Tim P.

How could anyone have known that through the simple act
of loving Tim we were in fact showing him Jesus Christ
and helping him to stay clean and sober? We are now
lovingly showing Jesus Christ to, oh some 15 addicts. They
are so precious! I love my daily walk with them. I have
loved them through jail, through rehab, through relapse and
through dragging them off the couch in a stupper. Now I
know just how God felt when He was loving me through all
my times.

The greatest spiritual experience(for me) through this has been during one of the worst; A man we had been ministering to for three months -who was doing so good- relapsed! Not only was he using again- he was GONE. And yet, two days latter he called the house and said

"I just want to come home."

That was awesome! God is good. And I also know the feelings behind the "parable of the prodigal son" Jesus told us about. To think or too believe that their is any other true source of power than a spiritual one is just plain wrong.

Natalie Taylor, Amarillo Texas

From the moment I entered recovery I have heard a lot about spiritual awakenings; people tell all about their first true "moment of clarity". This has always sounded so intriguing to me. It is so easy to get caught up in a hopeful fantasy of bright shining lights from above pouring down on us. Unfortunately, we may be waiting quite some time for a moment like that. My own misconceptions of a "spiritual awakening" had left me feeling disappointed. Then it happened; no not a shining light from heaven, not even a vision of God standing before me with words of wisdom. During one small bible study, a verse was read aloud that instantly answered so many of my questions I had about God and His ways. It was so unexpected, so quick that I could have very well missed it,(and I believe now so many do)had I not been listening. Then, suddenly, it happened again. A very close friend was sharing some literature that helped him in his recovery and BOOM, something clicked in my brain once again- another age old question was answered! The point is I (we) wasted so much time waiting on some miraculous heavenly explosion of some kind to count as a spiritual awakening only to discover that God speaks through real, normal, every day people. He speaks through literature and sermons as well. Little did I know, all I had to do is listen!

That Small Still Voice is God

Shelley Copeland, Dumas Texas

I grew up going to church with my family but my perception of God wasn't a comforting God. I always viewed God as a big man looking down at me pointing his finger at me saying "you messed up again." As I grew up, and had many life experiences, this perception only got worse.

Then through a life of addiction and several failed attempts at recovery I just knew I could never get to Heaven and that God could never forgive my sins because they were way to bad. However, in November of 2007, after another relapse I came to live at a place in Dumas, TX called The Refuge. I became involved with a group of people, most of them I had known all of my life, who showed me something I had never seen from anyone other than my immediate family, and that was love and acceptance. That Sunday I attended a church service with this same group of people who gathered around me, laid their hands on me and prayed that I know how much God loves me and that he forgives me for ALL of my sin. I never had any lightening bolts or burning bushes, but through prayers and bible studies I know that God does love me, that I am forgiven and I can forgive myself. Today my perception of God is a big man setting up in Heaven holding his arms out to inviting me to come set in his lap and let him be my rock. Thank you, Charles, my Refuge Family, and my church family for helping me find Gods love.

AGAPE LOVE of CHRIST

Steven Howell, Dumas Texas

I guess you could say I had hit a bottom. Being an addict for most of my life, I had hit many bottoms. Why was this one different? I had pulled all the strings, tried everything humanly possible and to place the icing on the cake, some fools were putting a recovery center across from my house? Go figure? I was at the point in my addiction where I was using drugs at a rate not humanly possible. I was in an $80k house with no electricity, no water and I was living in the garage with my dog. All I could do is feed my addiction. I had relationships but not really like most people did. It was strange, it was abusive yet, we couldn't seem to change. After one of these fights, I was walking away and I happen to pass this new recovery center being built. There, was an old friend, Wally, working on this building. I stopped, asked a few questions then went on. The new director, wasn't very talkative but my friend Wally was. I returned that evening and talked with the Director and that started my recovery.

Shortly after meeting these people for the first time, I was invited to a bible study at the Clark residence. Already seeing God at work, it just felt right to go to a strange person's house for a strange new activity. Go figure? There I found old friends and new. I seen people I had not seen in quite awhile, they were all clean, I suppose. At least they

88

were all searching for God. At the bible study, the Clarks always fed us.

It was probably the first real meal I had eaten in months. Not only was I being fed spiritually, I was feds physically. All that I can really remember is the food being good and the meeting ended on FAITH. I was told , " we know you do not have FAITH, so just have FAITH in us having FAITH!" I thought it strange that these people even cared? I would learn over the next few weeks that even more people cared and they did not judge me for what I had done. I attended church, I went to 12 step meeting and I made friends with people whom I would never expect. Before long God provided me with the funds to have our electric and water turned on. God also allowed me to begin being responsible with my tickets and warrants.

You would think that these people would abandon me if I relapsed: Nothing could be further from the truth! Through a loving God and loving people, I was sent to treatment in Lubbock Texas for 26 days. Each day letters came, people called and needs were met. These people, these church people, never once forgot me. They grew right along with me. They say that I help them as much as they help me, a concept still strange to me. How can I , an addict, a criminal, help anyone do anything? Yet through Jesus Christ we can all help each other learn just how to live life better.

Today, I am a different person. I have been born again! Oh, maybe not the born again as you think, but no doubt **'m a new person thru my Lord, Jesus Christ**

Dewayne Lunday, Duncanville Texas

Around May of 2001 I was awaiting sentencing on some serious charges in Dallas County jail. The night before I was to be sentenced I was talking to my cell mate about how worried I was about the outcome. I was looking at some serious jail time. He asked be If I believed in the Lord I told him I did but had not had any kind of relation-ship with him due to my drug use over the past 10 years. I really did not think God would or could help me because of how I have lived my life during my addiction. He told me before I went to bed to get on my knees and pray that God would help or show me what to do or say when I went before the D.A. That night I prayed for the first time in probably 10 years. When I finally fell asleep I had this calmness I had not felt in years. I had A dream that night that would change my life forever. The dream that God gave me went like this. I was working in my back yard at the house and there was some train tracks that ran behind my house and on the tracks was 1 locomotive with the number 2173 on the side of it.

I walked up to the train to investigate why it was just sitting there. I climbed onto the train and fell asleep, when I woke up the train was moving down the tracks and I did not know how to stop it. when I looked out I saw a brick wall I was about to hit. I finally got the train to stop right before it hit the wall. When I climbed of there was A dog on the other side of a fence barking at me. There was also a Two story brick ware house with ! door on the second story. All the sudden A man opened the door and said Son can I help you. I said yes I was on a runaway train and about to die. He said Son come up here And I will help you. Shortly there after I woke up.

I went to court the next morning and the D.A. gave me 5 years probation if I would sign some papers I agreed but when they passed me a pen it would not write. As they went back to get me another pen I remembered my dream and what my cell mate told me. He said there was a Rehab in Ft. Worth that sat right behind a lot of train tracks. At that moment I knew in my heart God wanted me to go there. I talked to the D.A. and he agreed to let me go. My first day there they toked me to the back and they had a dog that was running up and down a fence barking and when I looked over the fence there was 3 locomotives lined up and the lead one was 2173 just like my dream. after that i turned my life over to GOD and stayed clean for almost three yearning relapsed once when my mom passed away but with my belief in God and what he could do for me it was short lived.

There's a Long Black Train.........

Shannon Poole, Dumas Texas

My spiritual awakening came about 10 days or so after getting arrested in 2003. About half that time it took me to realize I was actually in jail. The other half I stayed as high as I was when I was on the streets. On April 22 2003 it came upon me that I had a problem -

> I was going to be 40 and I had nothing!
> (Sound familiar to anyone else?)

As I sat feeling sorry for myself, God sent a disciple to me. This one jailer was a warrior for Jesus Christ! He had already been there a couple of times; this time seem to be different?

I felt in my heart that I needed to listen to him. I was told that day " Jesus loves you and all you need to do is be quiet and listen to Him." I sat very still and just couldn't hear anything for a little while. But, then, as I sat there just holding my bible I heard " you are not alone and I will help you." I made a decision right there that i would not get high anymore. I threw everything I had away. I did not even open my bible that day but the next day and ever day since I have read it! I do not hear that same voice today; today it is a much clearer one!

Listen closely God doesn't Scream!

Thoughts and Ideas

Eternity, Infinity, Forever, Everlasting, Okay, we goofed! We humans had it all and we traded for what? Fruit! An apple? Okay, Okay, we actually traded it for knowledge, the knowledge of good and evil.

And just look at today. The exact same thing is true. We claim to pray, but to what? We attend church, but why? We even give our money, but for what reason?

American's can claim to be some of the best educated people on Earth, yet we do not know who we are or where we came from. If we are so smart, why do we continue to try and prove something that <u>must</u>be accepted on faith?

Let's take a quick look okay:

Higher Educated – # of years wasted in class

Political Correctness – lying by omission

Political Leaders – rich & famous "do-nothings"

Religious Fanatic – knows who he is & where he is.

So, exactly who needs to be leading and who needs to be following? For me, I TRY to follow the life and teachings of Jesus Christ. If his work is not enough then I simply find other humans who follow the same principles.

What principles? Spiritual Principles!

Which ones? All of them!

We find them everywhere:
From Paul's writings to the Galatians:From Bill Wilson's writings of the Big Book of A.A.;And from Jesus Christ himself we can conclude that there are some absolute spiritual principles and precepts needed for a Spiritual Awakening:

Honesty
   Willingness
      Integrity
      Love
         Hope
           Courage
           Faith
              Forgiveness
                  Compassion

Was 9/11 an act of God? No, I doubt it.

Was 9/11 an act of Satan? Maybe, yet I kind of doubt that too. 9/11 was an act of mean people. It was a very terrible thing. It was a shame all those people had to die. Still, it was just plain mean people. Mean people have been doing mean things since the beginning of time.

It's called free will! We all have it!

Were the Tsunamis an act of God? Maybe. They could have been, I guess. Or better yet, they may have been caused by all the drilling, digging, and mining done by human beings, but I doubt that too. Besides, like it or not, we re accountable to God! He is not accountable to us! We will never know in this world or the next if God caused them or not. We will never be given the opportunity to ask or put God on the spot. Those ideas are our arrogance.Look, it is my own belief that too often we are to quick to blame God and more often we are too quick giving Satan credit. Why can't we just accept that things happen?

ACCIDENTS DO HAPPEN, FOLKS!

That is unless you believe lawyers?
Why can't we understand that it is our choices that shape our tomorrows. It isn't always God, nor is it always Satan. Sometimes, most of the time, things just happen. And things happen to good people and bad, ok! Again we spend millions of dollars, thousand of hours trying to prove something that will <u>Never</u> be proven. Much of life <u>Must</u> be accepted on Faith.But hey, enough on all that! This idea for this book was more about my life and the journey toward the Light – Jesus Christ!

This book is about finding the Rock!

This book is about realizing we are human and although we

can strive to be perfect, we never will be (in this life). It takes a spiritual awakening to even get close, as you may have decided by this point And this book is about love! The love God has for us all. If we will just accept his gift of his son Jesus Christ.

Please go on, what have you got to loose ? See if maybe some of the stuff I have included here helps you with your own Spiritual Awakenings and progress. Each of us deals with our own form of addictions, food, alcohol, drugs, pornography, sex and cigarettes. So in fact we all need some sort of Spiritual Awakening to provide recovery and relapse prevention. Here is something I sincerely believe everyone can use.

PART FOUR

W.R.I.T.E.R.S

W illing

R eplies

I nitiated

T hrough

E motions

R elapes prevention made

S imple and easy

INTRODUCTION

Hello, my name is Charles Paul Stephens and I am the Executive Director of The Refuge @ Dumas. Also, I am a published author, speaker,facilitator, and a believe in Jesus Christ. Quite possibly I should have placed "believer in Christ"first today I do not mention them in order of actualimportance. Today, I need you to fully grasp the importance of writing and journaling as spiritual tools and ways to truly get to know Jesus Christ.The two(writing and journaling) are very differentyet equally important to spiritual growth.

This short work is designed help people with relapse prevention from whatever ails them.Yes, as you have already seen, we talk about God and Jesus. All I have is my experience ,strength and hope of 15 plus years of continuoussobriety. My one and only clean date is 11/11/01.

I thank God everyday for that and try my best tobe of maximum service to Him as an act of gratitude.

By writing and journaling you too can experiencesobriety along with peace and joy. It is my sincerestprayer that you will take this book and WORK IT! It is a WORK BOOK!

THEORIES AND OPINIONS

God wants our obedience not our vain sacrifices.Through prayer, meditation, writing and journalingwe show our true obedience to Him.

Through simple writing assignments we see just howwilling we are to reach out to God. through additionaljournaling we show our willingness to truly heal. We must be willing to take the smallest steps no matter how foolish or silly they seem.

My own personal experiences shows that writing relieves the pain of our past. By journaling we are far less likely to have those emotional eruptions that cause us so much pain and regret.

Writing freed me! and it can free you too! The simplest act of obedience toward God opens a door that no one can shut but us by stopping. God wants to helps us in our time of pain and struggle. He wants us to seek Him and writing is that path.

IN THE BEGINNING

We start with a simple Gratitude List. We make a easy one page list of those things we can be grateful for. Many of us are blinded by our circumstances or misfortunes and refuse to see what God does in our lives each and everyday. We must see the many gifts!

Things we ignore, like fresh air and fresh water; these are things many people in the world DO NOT have. Of course there are the small things like a toothbrush, or shampoo. And I doubt many us went without at least one or two meals today, no matter what our circumstance?

All of us at some point each day struggle with our emotions. Making a gratitude list helps us to see our circumstances more clearly. Remember our brains are not always our friends. Run on fear and control we make decision after decision that put us in a position of delusion or dream. We must face our reality!

God will show us the truth if we begin to see with our
HEARTS not our BRAINS

NEXT ON OUR LIST

If .....IF we are serious about our recovery we should now write a "Letter of Commitment" or "Contractual Agreement" This will outline exactly what we are willing to do to assure our personal recovery and healing process. It's your LIFE! Just how much are you committed to that life?

The "Letter of Commitment" should mention in specific terms what program(s) we are committed too and just how we will participate in those program(s). It should have a daily or weekly schedule of what we are truly willing to do too improve our own lives.

Last the contract should list any (all) questions that need to be ask prior to getting started. This is a life or death situation and we should consider it that. These questions should be about specific programs, daily scheduling and the all important prayer and meditation times.

God honors commitment; we must learn to honor it as well

A DAILY ADDITION

At this point, with commitment in hand, it is time to add another list to our daily agenda. On the back of our Gratitude List we need to begin writing a short Resentment List. Each evening(just before bedtime) we need to clear away our daily baggage(wreckage) This helps us to fully grasp the " One Day At a Time" attitude. We should always keep short accounts with God and with our fellows. It is so much easier to eat "hot crow" then it is to eat "cold or week old crow".

Going hour by hour, if need be, we review our day, seeking ANY anger or resentments. We remind our-selves that we need NOT carry senseless baggage into each new day. God said two things that pertain;

   1) "do not let the sun set on your anger"

2) "do not sin while in your anger"

Of course I am paraphrasing thus leaving you too find these two great verses in the near future. It just might be on a test at some point. Hint; I sincerely believe they are both in the New Testament.

DO ONE OF THE TWO

At this point in time you should have somewhere between 30 and 45 days and I give you the option of which new assignment you would like to do. Both are simple, neither are very easy.

>   a. continue on writing(as you are) only now begin a complete life story starting at your earliest memory.

Write down most everything that crosses your mindas important, especially those resentments and regrets.

>   b. take 3x5 cards in the same number as your age. 30 years old equals 30 cards. Begin listing everything you can remember on a card - one year, one card. Begin with your very first memory and move forward till today.

Which ever you do, it should take one day per year to complete. If you are 30, it should take 30 days to finish.

Likewise with 20 years and 20 day. As I said, this is a very simply assignment yet it is not very easy. Oh and do not forget, this should fit into your day without neglecting ANY of your previous commitments.

REFLECTIONS

This is the place in our walk where we stop and reflect on exactly what we have done. Did we put enough effort into our writing? Were we honest in all areas? Did we leave out part parts that were uneasy or uncomfortable thus lying by omission? Remember; **We are only as sick as our secrets**

Looking back, what could we have done better? Where could we have placed just a little extra effort to help our healing process? Did we put in enough yeast(activator) to cause the dough(healing) to rise? Only you and God know for sure. Take just a few moments and reflect on your commitment and performance; make any additions you need to once and for all - **ACTIVATE HEALING.**

ACTIVATE HEALING NOW

We have ALL been hurt! Some have had broken bones while others have had broken hearts. Many have gone to doctor while others MUST stay in the hospital. All of us have been hurt in one form or another. Most of us have the scars to prove that we have been hurt. Me, I have many scars, both, internally and externally. This is why we must be willing to do anything to Activate healing.

Once we begin writing we stop wasting so much time thinking. Instead we are taking action against our hurts. By getting honest and willing our brains can no longer use our hurts to destroy us or render us useless through mental illness like depression.

Looking back, our list are the keys to our hurts that are still hurting. We seek out each of those and list the people who are involved. We simply make the list, we do NOT seek them out by phone or in person. This is NOT the time for apologies, that comes later.

The list, the people, the places and the hurts, are the keys to Activate Healing Now.

HAND WRITTEN LETTERS

It wasn't that long ago that ALL letters were hand written. Just a decade, maybe two prior everyone had to hand write letters if they wanted to communicate. The healing that came with that (quite possibly) is why so many of these folks remained married for 30-40-50 years. Not to mention the dramatic lack of suicides in that same group.

Possibly, just as important and healing, were the 1000s of handwritten letters during wartime that were never mailed. These acted as "outlets" for those folks who could have gotten lost down the highway of drugs and/or alcohol.

Today, just as then, take your list that you made from the previous work and begin writing a letter to each person, one person at a time, one week at a time. Be careful not to loose track or forget who you are dealing with. Remember, we are Dealing with Healing, your healing. So play close attention to detail as you write each letter to each person.

Try to leave each letter in a notebook so you actually see the habits and cycles of hurt. If you must, due to content, place the letter in an envelope with only the first name on the front. Never address it and never mail it until you have talk with a trusted friend or advisor. We should NEVER hurt anyone for our own good. Replacing one hurt for another gets us nowhere.

MY PRAYER FOR EACH

It is my prayer and my hope that by this time each of you has the desire(habit) to journal everyday, in addition to your written list. My prayer is that God has began His miracles of healing inside of you and you are desiring even more.

The freedom and relief that comes with daily writing and journaling is beyond compare. The simplest act Activates Healing and begins a life-long process of obedience to God and the healing that come with that.

Journaling is the medicine, the balm, the soothing salve that we put on our scars. This medicine softens our scars(heart) and healing start. Scars are layers of tissue that form to protect a wound.

Our scars are the same, layers of emotion and fear that

protect us from the world and other people. Only things is, they also keep us from love; the love of God and the love of friends. By journaling we can soften the scars, begin the healing and truly learn how to love again.

*And the greatest of these is LOVE *

THE POWER OF LOVE

What is love? Who defines love? How, exactly do we know love? We can look at John 3:16 or 1st Corinthian 13 of the Bible and get an idea about love. Yet, who can really understand the love of one person laying down their life for another?

Here try these, maybe they will help a little;

a)	b)	c)
L.isten	L.earn	L.ustful
O.bserving	O.beying	O.bessive
V.isual	V.irtuous	V.ictory
E.xciting	E.nergetic	E.nvious

See the difference in what we think and what we know? Which one of these sounds the best to you? Surely you would pick a) or b) and not c)?

The key to LOVE (I believe) is another word that is seldom used and never really understood -HONOR! A second word is RESPECT! Both great words, both needed for LOVE and both can be very disagreeable when used wrong or with malice.

Your writing assignment here is NOT to define LOVE but to define all the words associated with LOVE. You search your heart, you pick the words and you define each of them as best possible.

Please do not insult yourselves by using definition straight from the dictionary, ok.

A RETURN TO LOVE

Thousands of books have been written about love. Literally thousands, maybe millions of sermons have been preached on love. Yet LOVE still eludes many of us. Why? Could it be that (in our minds) most of us have love and lust all messed up? We have all seen or heard the root - Eros, Phileo and Agape. The first being the love from sight or lust, the second being love for brother to sister or army buddies one to another and the last being the love of a mother to her new born child or that of a father to a new born son.

*Love is a verb not a noun or a pronoun *

Now, what do I mean by that? We cannot speak love, we must show love. And we do not show love through sex but by every action and every word we have for each other.

Here we want to list(write) about the ways we know how to show love. We try our best to avoid the sex and stick to just agape love. We may have to use our moms, dads or children to try and fill this list. It is my guess that this WILL NOT be easy since most of us have Sex and Love all messed up!

LOVE SCRIPTURES

Mark 12:31

The second is this: '**Love** your neighbor as **yourself**.' There is no commandment greater than these."

loves you because you have loved me and have believed that I came from **God**.

comes from **God**. Everyone who **loves** has been born of **God** and knows **God**.

And he has given us this command: Whoever **loves God** must also love his brother
John 3:16

For God so loved the world that he gave his one and only Son, that whoever believes in him shall not perish but have eternal life.

Yes , you do have *__rights__*.

you have the **Right.**.......

> to be angry.............................
> to be mad ....
> to be abusive ....
> even to be rageful ....
or.......... You can chose LOVE!

Are you willing to suffer the consequences for hate?

Every chose you make, every mistake you make, has a **real Consequence**

What are some of those consequences you have already felt?

> 1)_____
> 2)_____
> 3)_____
> 4)_____

Other people have rights too,

We can LOVE or We can HATE
We can either RESENT or
We can FOREGIVE:
those are our only real choses!

PART FIVE

THE FRUIT AND THE VINE SYNOPSIS

Many of you may have read a book called "The Secrets of the Vine?" by Wilkerson. I know I did & I enjoyed the reading very much as a young believer. However today I find myself at odds with it's teachings. I sincerely believe that Jesus did not mean anything to be a secret. Quit the opposite, He wanted us first to develop a relationship with Him , then He would revel a "Map" to the kingdom of heaven. The story He tells in that map. A clear cut, easy to read map to God and to Heaven. And yes while we are on this earth a map to Life as only Jesus meant for it to be!

Although I firmly believe that spiritual principles are never in conflict, that they truly will compliment each other, I do believe that we are given interpretations that do conflict.

The Bible itself is the Word Of God , given by God to man and I believe that the bible is true and left to no interpretation at all. This book, the actual story that Jesus told is in John Chapter 15. the story He tells is the last "teaching" to the disciples before

His crucification.

It is meant to show us the exact relationship we are suppose to have with Him, Jesus and with Him, God! Make no mistake it is the road map to a wonderful future. Over the years the church and many of it's pastors have painted a picture that "The fruit or a person's fruit" equates to more people. As I study this scripture, as I grow to know the Lord I come to the conclusion that this cannot be right. Actually it may be partially right? But it must first be put into context. A text with out a context is a pretext. Thus incomplete.

We see this same example repeat itself through out the churches. If we look at the many "End-Time-Profits" we see them telling about all the prophecy that is coming true. Yet they all fail to include what Jesus said " I will come as a theft in the night!" Does anyone ever know when a theft is going to rob? Jesus also tells the story of coming for His bridesmaid. If we look at this tradition we see that the bride is hid and the groom comes for when no one knows except himself. Now here are two very well penned examples that show we, as humans will Never know the time or the hour of Jesus coming. So claiming to know or understand cannot be the complete truth.

Yet the true qualifying statement to this whole affair and yes to the book in whole is the statement that Paul makes in

Galatians where he list the "fruit of the spirit"! Fruit of the spirit, wow! Here we are given a complete list of " the fruit" and told that there is "no law against these"! This in itself should show that "the fruit" are indeed more than people. The fruits of the spirit are the fruit of the vine! And they are ours, intended for us to use to glorify our Lord Jesus.

Paul also warns us against the misrepresentation of scripture. He warns that we may even be approached by an angel of light (satan) and told that things are true when in fact they are false! I myself, refuse to change the scripture, I read them as they are written and I let God interpret them for me. I sincerely believe this is the only way to the truth.

How many of you have ever seen and actual vineyard? A real life vineyard with the rows and rows of vines (or trunks)held up by a long trellis. Some may have a single trellis for each vine(trunk) that comes out of the ground. The roots of the vine(trunk) are what gives the vine and it's branches water and nutrition. As the nutrition is spread from the vine it begins to grow branches. And in most cases the vines are cut back each year to the trunk because ONLY new vines produces fruit each year.

Jesus said " I am the vine, you are the branches and God is the vine-dresser or husbandman." So Jesus is the vine, the trunk, the Provider! We are the branches, the limbs, the part of the plant that holds the leaves and grows the fruit. What fruit? The fruit of the spirit as defined in Galatians by Paul.

God, the husbandman or gardener then prunes or trims the branches (us) so that we will produce more fruit! What fruit? Not People ,the fruit of the spirit, right? What else could it be? Nowhere in the writing does it say that "the fruit" are people. The passage that says " Go Forth and be fruitful" does not equate to people.

Branch cannot move about. Branches are not suppose to move, they are joined to the vine, Jesus! And what is Jesus? The Church! Neither the branches nor the fruit can go forth they are attached to the vine, Jesus! This brings us to harvest time!

Once we are fruitful, once the fruit becomes ripe, then we need labor. We need harvesters and pickers to gather the fruit. These people are usually transits or migrant workers, the poor and needy of our communities, that come to each vineyard in time to gather the perfect fruit for market. This brings us to yet another participate, the merchant or the vendor!He is the person that buys the fruit and takes it out into the world!

The Evangelist

So we have the harvesters or disciples who gather the fruit and they present it to the merchant or vendors, the evangelist and they are the ones who present it to the world at large. We, the church are only responsible for staying close to Jesus, staying attached to the vine, our provider, so that we may produce a bountiful crop for the merchants to distribute to the rest of the world.

Now does that sound more like it? The pretense that We, the branches are to separate from the vine and go forth to bear our fruit is totally impossible! We the branches stay close to Jesus, our Provider, our nutritionist, to remain fruitful! We cannot "go forth" and in fact were never suppose to "go forth".

This was a ploy to help fill the churches with non-believers. Throughout the ages the church has been known to preach a certain way or act a certain simply to attract a new group of people. A term feel-good-church has developed from that.

All they care about is that each member leaves each Sunday feeling good! Well, again nowhere in God's word does He worry about how we feel! He cares about what we are DOING.

Then we have the works churches who believe that all we have to do is good works. If we just do right then we will all be saved. Again I say , nowhere in God's word is this written! The 5 acts of worship are useless if we are NOT fulfilling His commandments.

Jesus clearly tells us that there are jobs for everyone. Not everyone is meant to be a preacher, not everyone will be an evangelist. But everyone can be a branch and everyone can bear fruit! All they have to do is stay attached to the vine, stay close to Jesus, Period! There will be the pickers, the gathers, the preachers and the evangelist that will gather the fruit and go forth with it! Praise God for these people. They are the ones that will bring in the new branches and thus more fruit will be grown and more fruit can be distributed among the ones who actually need it(the fruit).

We as church members are the branches. We are connected to each other through Jesus, the Vine, The Provider! God hereby deals with each of us by pruning and trimming so they we produce more fruit! What Fruit? The fruits of the spirit as Paul list them in Galatians. The fruit then attracts people to us! First the harvesters then the merchants and vendors.

They go forth and say..............

"Wow have you ever seen so much fruit?"

"Say where did that great fruit come from?"

"Wow, I really would like to have some of that fruit!"And from these events come more people and more people equal more branches and that equals even more fruit for the glory of the church , Jesus!

If....IF we have the best fruits, if we have the grandest harvest then we attract more people. If we separate ourselves we wither and we die. Which would you prefer?Better fruit attracts more people! What fruit? The fruits of the spirit as list in Galatians by Paul!

Many churches may not want to believe this. Especially if said church has a large number of members who possess little or no fruit. As well if a church is in turmoil or disention the same may be true; they may have little or no fruit! For them, it is much easier to have a revival or growth campaign then to actually obtain the fruits of the spirit. Today the big push is Purpose! Churches across the nation are having their members find there purpose? Why? Jesus gave us our purpose " to produce much fruit!" Why not follow Jesus' instruction, accept God's pruning and produce the fruit needed to attract people to the church? What other purpose is there?

What other purpose is needed?

Well to do that we must look inside not outside! it is so much easier to focus our energies outside than it is for us to look inside ourselves! It is so much easier to place blame or point fingers than it is to look deep down inside or own souls! Folks, please believe me, it is not about "them"! The "them" of this world are not our problems!

We are our major problem! Flesh!

WE all make mistakes

It does not mean we are not a mistake

God does NOT make mistakes or trash

"We Praise Him when we win – We Praise Him when we lose"

Here are a few scriptures that might help;

Therefore, as **God's** chosen people, holy and dearly **loved**, clothe yourselves with compassion, kindness, humility, gentleness and patience.

Is there anything of which one can say, "Look! This is something new"?

It was here already, long ago; it was here before our time.

For from within, out of men's hearts, come evil thoughts, **sexual immorality**, theft, murder, adultery,

List Several(4-5)mistakes you have made
1)_____
2)_____
3)_____
4)_____

Do you believe Jesus died so you are Forgiven

We are all creatures of habit. We must change our thinking to change habits:

Our Thinking determines Our Choices.....

Our Choices define Our Habits...............

Our Habits develop Our Character............

Our Character delivers Our Destiny.........

Our Destiny determines Our HOPE........

HOPE is what makes LIFE worth living!

*Stinking Thinking Gives Us A Smelly Future!

2 Timothy 4: 1 – 5
I give you this charge: 2Preach the Word; be prepared in season and out of season; correct, rebuke and encourage—

with great patience and careful instruction. 3For the time will come when men will not put up with sound doctrine. Instead, to suit their own desires, they will gather around them a great number of teachers to say what their itching ears want to hear. 4They will turn their ears away from the truth and turn aside to myths. 5But you, keep your head in all situations, endure hardship, do the work of an evangelist, discharge all the duties of your ministry

---

Ye shall know the truth, and the truth shall make you free.
John 8:32

Not only that, it will set those around you FREE!

CLOSURE

Proverbs 22: v 28 "Remove not the ancient landmarks, which thy fathers have set."

America is dead set against its Godly heritage. We have already begun the prophesy of Proverbs 22:28. From removing the Ten Commandments from every government building, too excluding prayer from schools and office, we are removing the landmarks of our fore-father. America is wrong in its definition of church and state!

We have allowed liberal judges to change this God loving, God fearing nation! "Separation of church" was to secure religious future. This religious freedom was for <u>ALL</u>! It does mean we can remove the landmarks left as examples of this freedom by our fore-fathers. Instead, what has happened is biblical prophesy.

The Ten Commandments are removed, crosses are being banned, yet, Muslims still wear their brightly colored ceremonial clothing, and the Jewish still get to wear their little religious hats and why?

How fair is this? I am at odds how we will live into the next century. In a civilized country, with so called religious freedom, will we begin to remove crossed from cemeteries? Will we remove brick and stone with scriptures from buildings too? And will we destroy churches with ANY outward wording ?

Are we going to continue this perverted interpretation of independence? Will we eventually remove God from every piece of our great history? This is a serious prophesy. We are in serious violation of biblical law.

Will we continue to destroy the examples and truths our fore-fathers left for us? Have we become Babylon?

Or will we check our conscience, check our motives and return to the education of our earlier life? Believe it or not God is real! And the Biblical truths of an earlier era are just as real. Religious leaders right along side political leaders are making some big mistakes.

Mistakes that are leading us down roads we could avoid.

Hopefully, this book will help others to have their own spiritual awakenings. Awakenings that will direct their actions over the next decade or so. We need to re-unite the church and the nation. As long as we are fight among ourselves, as long as we argue over denominational doctrine, America will NEVER heal. Stop, think, and listen

- God is easy to find!

All we have to do is enter into quite meditation and He will always present Himself to us. May you have the most awesome Spiritual Awakening Ever! And may you find , as I did, that sharing it is the best way to live!

In Loving Service To Jesus

Charles Paul Stephens

Dumas Texas 2007 - 08

COMMEMORATIVE PAGE

In an attempt to be many things to many people I often fail. It is "those people" that I wish to reconize at this time and in this way; In life, we are given the chance to serve others. We can either accept that service or we can pass. Over the years, many people have served me on my spiritual walk. I simply could not make it had it not been for their service.

Pastor Parkey Cobern, Fort Worth Texas
Pastor Tim and Pam H. Wichita Falls TX.
Bruce Cameron LPC, Fort Worth Texas
Danne Pearn, Duininck Brothers N. Texas
Chris Terry and Family, Fort Worth Texas
The late Gene Reynolds Fort Worth Texas

The only thing we know about Jesus is written by men who were inspired by the Holy Spirit. Maybe all we will ever know about these men is what I write about them being inspired as well by the same Holy Spirit. God Bless you all for all you did.

Thank you Lord Jesus for all you have done for me, in Life, in Marriage and in Career! What can I do to be of service today?

Your Servant
Charles

Printed in the United States
149398LV00001B/44/P

9 781432 720964